FROM BROKE TO BANK: STEP BY STEP GUIDE TO YOGA MARKETING CONSULTING BUSINESS

Soham M.

Copyright © 2018

All rights reserved. No part of this book may be reproduced or transmitted in any form or by any means, electronic or mechanical, including photocopying, recording or by any information storage and retrieval system without written permission of the publisher, except for the inclusion of brief quotations in a review.

Disclaimer:

Please read the Disclaimer carefully before you read this book. You accept and agree to be bound and abide by the Disclaimer. The information contained on this book is for educational and informational purposes only. The information contained on this book is not intended as, and shall not be understood or construed as, professional advice. This book should be treated as fictional account.

The brand names or logos discussed in this book are property of their respective owners.

Before approaching the client 6
Understanding your role as a marketing consultant 8
Why your client needs you. 10
Market research 12
Planning for Hiring 14
Know your team 16
Increasing Presence on Social Media 18
The power of testimonials 24

The business that this book discusses is the job as a marketing consultant for Yoga Center. This book explores the role of marketing consultant in formulating the strategies that can handle the brand value as well as attract new customers for the Yoga Center. Some people argue that the business of yoga center is highly localized and does not require marketing consultant because people have the notion that local businesses do not require specialized marketing. This is incorrect because local business requires more focus and laser targeted approach to reach potential clients.

Before approaching the client

Before approaching the client you must make adequate preparations like fine-tuning your sales script. If you have any apprehension about approaching the customer or are afraid to do the cold calling for prospecting the clients, then you must practice rehearsing your sales script for few times.

Before approaching the client the following points must be kept in mind while drafting a sales script. Your new sales script must have a decent opener because many people fumble in the opening sentences, you have to become different in your approach, many people try to play word games before broaching the subject of marketing consultancy, tell your client that you are meeting them because you have a solution to offer for their business. Many people hide their intentions for the fear of agitating the client, this is a wrong approach. You have to be very clear about your intentions to establish a business relationship.

To practice the sales script, you can request one of your friends to become a dummy customer so that you can give your sales presentation. You can get a feedback from your friend regarding your sales presentation, whether it requires modifications or tweaking a bit. You must also avoid making unnecessary gestures that might make you appear to be aggressive. While writing the sales script keep in mind that you will be required to lead the client in the conversation, so make sure to list all possible objections that your client might have including "I do it myself" excuse. Remember that your sales script is your first and last opportunity to demonstrate to your client about your authority in marketing. In the first meeting with your client, you might have to convince him about the benefits that you can provide for his business, the various marketing strategies you can help with including digital marketing, etc. In making these efforts you might not be successful in making the client agree for business. Do not show any sign of disappointment and maintain a pleasant attitude at all times. You might have to call 4-5 times, follow it up regularly with the client and look carefully for any sign that he might be interested in a particular topic. Suppose a client is interested only in local business then you can grab this opportunity to show him how you can help him to grow his business locally.

Understanding your role as a marketing consultant

Your role as a marketing consultant for a client or local business is to formulate online as well as offline marketing strategies. You may have to work with a project team consisting of a copywriter, a photographer, the web designer, etc. you will also be required to liaison between the project team and a client.

You are the key between the client and the project team, because they are dependent on you for guidance, if you are unavailable or are unable to guide them then the project team might not know what to do, and this can crash the entire marketing campaign. You'll have to constantly monitor the marketing campaign or social media to optimize the return on investment for your client. You will have to keep a check on the expenditure and ensure that there is no overspending.

You will be required to offer flexible marketing options to your client. you must have the knowledge of content marketing and paid marketing on platforms like Facebook, viral marketing, creation of the word of mouth buzz, reaching out to local customers, etc. you will also be required to help your client to identify the niche if he has not done already. You will be required to help your client build an online presence through website, Facebook pages or videos. You must also assist your client in his networking efforts to grow their business, and formulate a strategy for increasing presence on social media. You will also have to identify the local events that can help your client to gain mileage in terms of building a brand value and getting new customers.

Why your client needs you.

Just because you have the knowledge of marketing tactics is not enough reason for your client to trust you. You must be well prepared when you approach the client and for this purpose, before approaching a client you must carry out a little research. This will demonstrate your commitment to your work. You can prepare a free report for your prospective client, it must not be a lengthy report, but you could research the client's website if he has one and if he doesn't have a website then you must make a note of this specifically. There are several website analysis tools available for free that can analyze the website content including the use of keywords, placement of keywords, loading time of website, whether the website is optimized for mobile, etc. You can also spend some time to research if your clients business has any kind of reviews on the internet and make a note of them. If your client does not have reviews on the internet then you can highlight this as an important task that needs to be accomplished. If your client is operating a local business, you can perform a check whether his business appear in the search or is the business information up to date on search engines. You can also spend some time to research if the client has a presence on Facebook, if he has a presence then you can analyze his page and identify the weaker elements that needs to be improved. You can also check the frequency of updates and mention it in your report, if the updates are not done at regular intervals. This report will show your commitment to your work and your client will certainly appreciate if you point out the weaknesses in his marketing strategy and suggest ways to improve it. You can also point out to your client that the traditional methods of marketing like billboards or attending the trade shows, while they are important there are digital channels that your client must pursue. Your client must keep up with the latest trends and embrace of marketing strategy that can deliver maximum returns on investment. You can also stress on hiring the expert in every area of marketing, which might not be available to the client if he decides to implement the strategy on his own. You can stress that you as a marketing consultant have access to the right tools and the right people for making a business successful. The most important reason to hire you as a marketing consultant is that the owner can focus on his core business that is yoga and his focus on his core business will lead to higher customer satisfaction that will benefit his brand indirectly.

Market research

Now that your client has appointed you as a marketing consultant your first priority is to identify the strengths and weaknesses of your client's business. You will have to prepare the list of competitors and the services offered by them including the special offers if any. You will be required to make a comparison chart of the services offered by your client and his competitors, and have to analyze the market segment that your client is in. You will have to identify the core areas that your client could operate in without sacrificing the quality of the service being offered, for example, your client's Yoga Center offers services only for females for weight loss then you have to explore if there is a room for adding new products such as Yoga training for kids, yoga for the elderly that specifically targets particular disease. you can even explore if your client can offer therapeutic yoga. After making the list of the services that could be offered by the yoga center and the services offered by your client you can have a discussion about expanding the business.

You can help your client to find out the value that can be delivered in their business if your client wants to offer weight loss services. You, as a marketing consultant, can explore additional avenues to increase profitability and attract new customers, is it possible to offer special yoga classes to other group of people, or explore the options of selling courses related to yoga or CDs, this kind of brainstorming can result in the development of new products that can eventually result in an increase in business for your client.

You will also need to visit other Yoga Center that offer weight loss programs to their clients and prepare a comprehensive list of their offerings. You might even have to register on your client's competitor's websites to check for periodical offers for new as well as existing customers and keep track of such offers

If your client wants to focus on the local market then your internet strategy also has to be geared to achieve the goal.

Planning for Hiring

As a Freelancer, you must plan for the expansion and recruitment of employees beforehand. If you plan to recruit workers then you have to adhere to this section. Employees, both contractual and a permanent may be redeemed through internet job sites, placing an ad in local newspapers. The hiring is a slow process, typically you will not be recruiting people en masse, and the hiring will be contingent on the expansion of your organization. Additionally, you need to have a clearly defined role for an employee which aligns with your organization's vision.

If your business is expanding, it is a good sign, but you must carefully plan the recruitment procedure, this way you'll have ample time to choose the candidates which could prove to be the assets of the company. It is completely normal to experience some stress when are hiring for the very first time. However, the hiring additionally expects that you, as an entrepreneur must be aware of certain laws since you don't want any problems on the front. It might be that you might not require the full-time employee; however the misclassification between an employee and an independent contractor might have grave consequences.

This is mandatory as it assists the income tax department to ascertain whether the tax obligations are fully satisfied. As soon as you've obtained EIN, you can make an application for worker withholding tax.

One other important matter to consider while hiring a worker is to be sure you are hiring a person who's qualified to work your country. Every new employee is required to sign firm I-9 together with the required documents. After you complete the above formalities, you can issue a job offer letter which spells the project description along with terms of job. As your company grows, you will also demand a payroll provider to maintain normal records.

Once you hire an employee, you'll be asked to withhold the taxes from the paychecks of their employees. As an entrepreneur you must have the knowledge of W-4 and W-2 forms.

In Case you have hired an employee, then it is a good idea to have the IRS form W-4 filled out by your workers before they receive their first paycheck. You Need to maintain the records of the tax withholding or provide However, you must remember that the W-4 Form has to be filled only once by a worker until his tax status changes.

Know your team

If your client has a website then its fine, if he doesn't have a website then you have to work with a web developer. Keep in mind that the website must not be cluttered with unnecessary information. The feel of the website must be aesthetically appealing. Think of the website as the face of the company. The layout of the website must be simple and it must be easy to navigate different sections of the website.

You will also be working with the copywriter or creative writing. The job of creative writing is to create the compelling copy that attracts the attention of the customer. If you observe the television ad or the print ad then you will notice that these advertisements are designed to appeal to the consumer emotionally, the advertisements are never designed to appeal to the logic of a person. A good creative writer knows that words have the power to appeal to the emotions and if an advertisement is successful in connecting with the customer emotionally then there are high chances of the customer buying the product.

A graphic designer is another member of the team that is very important because if the website has poor graphics then it might become a turn off for the customer. The pictures of the yoga sessions or about the yoga facility must be visually appealing to the customers. It is a known fact that visually appealing pictures are shared more on the social media websites. A visually appealing picture along with a good and creative copy can attract customers very easily.

You will be closely working as a liaison between your client and the team. You have to guide your team to obtain the maximum results for your client. You must also have regular brainstorming sessions with your team to optimize the campaigns that are launched by you. You will need to closely monitor the response of the customers and will have to respond to their queries.

You will also have to report your client every week about the progress of the campaigns. You can eliminate the campaigns that not working after consultation with your client.

Increasing Presence on Social Media

Facebook is an excellent platform to reach your potential customers even if the business of your client is highly localized. This is because Facebook allows you to Target the specific customers in the specific location. You can leverage the power of Facebook to increase your social reach.

Since the business of Yoga Center is highly localized, it would be advised able to design the campaign that focuses on the local market.

You can design custom offers, or organized contest like creating a catchy slogan for your studio, sharing the experiences of the customers on Facebook and rewarding them with special discounts, this kind of steps go long way in building customer awareness about the Yoga center and creating customer satisfaction.

You can even advice your client to organize community-based challenge for yoga classes, for example, if the person is willing to take the challenge then he can participate in the challenge and post regular updates on your clients Facebook page. This will generate a constant stream of interaction between your existing and new customers. Always remember that the majority of the success of the fitness industry depends on the word of mouth publicity generated by the customers themselves.

You can even advise your clients to offer corporate wellness programs because today more and more companies are becoming aware of maintaining the fitness of their employees. Companies have begun to understand that if the employees are healthier then they will be attending the office regularly and will have the greater stamina that will eventually benefit the company.

You can even emphasize on group yoga sessions for the employees of the company, usually, many companies have stationery fitness equipment installed for their employees but they remain unused for the lack of motivation. If the yoga center can offer discounts for group yoga sessions then the employees might also get the required motivation to attend the classes. Group yoga sessions can also help the company to build a good rapport amongst its employees. You can even suggest an innovative pricing strategy like charging for hourly group sessions instead of charging individually. This type of innovative pricing can be instrumental in creating a positive buzz amongst corporate clients.

Every business has a competitor who offers innovative solutions to their clients. You must advise your client to have a unique selling proposition that can attract customers. The yoga center can offer a free trial session or tie-up with online coupon sites to offer a trial coupon to the customers. This will enable the people to purchase a $5 coupon to attend a trial yoga class and experience the services themselves.

The most important sales people for the business are the customers themselves. There is nothing great then customer talking positively about the business. It is very difficult to convert customers into the brand ambassadors of the business because only those companies succeed in converting the customer into a brand ambassador who offers exceptional customer service at the most competitive prices to their customers.

The yoga center must always listen to what their clients want, great products are usually created by the customers themselves. You can also encourage your client to allow the customers to bring their friends for trial sessions. This gesture will help you to spread the word about the yoga center in the particular locality and effectively advertise its services. Yoga center can even bundle an offer by offering the trial access to other packages of the center, this way if the customer who does not intend to buy other packages will become aware of the same packages by trying themselves.

If something is done for the community then it goes along way in creating the brand value for the company. For example, if the studio is located near an elderly home then free sessions could be arranged for the elders, they can be educated about the benefits that yoga provides for them as a senior citizen.

The price structure could be designed in such a way that it benefits every class of the customer that want to be a part of the yoga centre. For example, discounts could be offered to the students who want to join the yoga centre. Students usually depend upon their parents and if the packages are specifically tailored for students in such a way that it does not hurt their pocket then they could become not only a good source of revenue but they can spread the word about the yoga center very quickly. This will also help to fill any vacant slots that the yoga center might have.

You can even encourage the yoga center to post the pictures and videos of the center. Videos have a huge impact in attracting the clients; yoga center can demonstrate its uniqueness and expertise by the use of videos. The customer can be educated about the various yoga poses and the benefit they offer. People practice yoga because their goal is to remain fit and healthy, with the help of videos the yoga center can demonstrate the health benefits of each pose, and the relief it provides in various illnesses. This kind of education can increase the confidence of the customer in the yoga centre, and they might be tempted to try the yoga centre.

The best way to create a positive word-of-mouth publicity for the yoga center is to post the pictures of happy customers practicing yoga. The yoga center can even encourage customer to post their pictures in the yoga center on their social media accounts and for doing so the yoga center can offer a special rebate to those customers. Even if 50 customers post such pictures and videos in their respective accounts then it can reach the wide audience and increase curiosity among the prospective clients.

It is also important to track what people saying about the yoga center on the internet. A person might post a positive or negative review about the yoga centre, it is very important to interact with such reviews because many business owners make the mistake of ignoring such reviews, this not only sounds arrogant but reinforces the notion that the business does not care about its customers. Even if somebody has posted a negative review about the yoga center on the internet then it is advisable that the center does not react in a negative way, any response to the negative comments must be offer in a soft tone by apologizing for the inconvenience caused to the customer. The same customer should be invited again to visit the yoga center either for free or offering a sizeable discount. Admitting the mistakes will create an image that the yoga center cares for its customers which in turn well give a boost to the prospective customers. In fact, if there is a slightest opportunity to interact with the customers then it must be welcomed with open arms because it is an opportunity to showcase that the yoga center cares for its customers and this is the message that must be passed to the customer.

There must also be a referral program for the customers, and tangible benefits like discounts or free courses should be offered to them as an incentive. If the customer does something for the center either by way of referring someone or by posting anything positive on the social media then he must be rewarded in some form. The customers are a valuable asset and they must be delighted at every available opportunity.

A local radio station is also the best way to reach a potential customer. Each radio station has a channel that is less popular and this is where the yoga center must focus for advertising. It is possible to get a good bargain for the air time in a less popular channel. The yoga center can focus on the linear advertisements offered by the radio channel. In Linear advertisement, the radio announcer reads the message of the advertiser. The biggest advantage of the linear advertisement is that it makes it look like it has been endorsed by the celebrity i,e, the radio announcer. This could provide a big boost to the perceived brand value of the yoga centre.

The yoga centre can even organize seminar or free webinars. These seminars can be organized to educate the people about various avenues that available for local businesses. This type of free seminar is great way to win the confidence of the people because they establish one as an authority in the industry. People appreciate those who share their expertise and knowledge, and sharing of knowledge increases the credibility of the yoga centre. If the yoga centre is able to establish them as a authority then it will make people feel safe to utilize their services.

Seminar are also the best way to showcase various products that can help individuals reach their goals for example there could be a person who wants to get rid of the joint pain, the seminar is a great way to demonstrate how yoga can help to ease his joint pain, similarly a person who is experiencing stiffness in the body can see how yoga can help his body to become flexible. Seminars are a great way to demonstrate the benefits of various products and services that the yoga centre offers.

Seminar also offers an excellent opportunity to interact with the potential customers of the yoga centre. By answering the questions personally one can remove any doubt that a person might have about the services offered by the yoga centre. This kind of question- answer session can also help to develop close connection between the yoga centre and the prospective customer.

The power of testimonials

What is the first thing one notice while visiting a yoga center or a fitness center, the people who are doing exercises, their passion tells a lot about the center and its ambience. If people not happy, they would not enjoy doing something.

The power of testimonials can never be underestimated. A company receives testimonial only when it has consistently delivered value in terms of products and services to the customer. If the Yoga Centre provides excellent service then there will be people who will happily testify for them. People will trust a testimonial even if it comes from the complete stranger. No amount of advertising budget can equal the power of a testimonial. The Yoga Centre must ask its clients periodically if they would like to offer a written or video testimonial if they are satisfied with the services. If the client has benefited by utilizing the services of the Yoga Centre then he will have no problem providing a testimonial.

People are visual creatures so if the testimonial is in the video form it will greatly increased its power. Videos have the power to make the people feel various emotions of the speaker. These emotions could be happiness, excitement, contentment, etc. Videos also have a longer retention span thus a viewer will immediately recollect the name of the yoga Centre as soon as he sees on the internet. Frequently collections of the brand can lead to the familiarity and increased perception about the brand, which will benefit the yoga center in the long run.

More Books In The Series

STEP BY STEP GUIDE TO SURVIVE AS COPYWRITER

STEP BY STEP GUIDE TO PET SITTING BUSINESS

STEP BY STEP GUIDE TO DIGITAL MARKETING CONSULTING BUSINESS

STEP BY STEP GUIDE TO DENTAL CLINIC MARKETING CONSULTING BUSINESS

STEP BY STEP GUIDE TO RESAURANT MARKETING CONSULTING BUSINESS

www.ingramcontent.com/pod-product-compliance
Lightning Source LLC
Chambersburg PA
CBHW031525210526
45464CB00007B/3025